PRESENTED TO:

_____

FROM:

_____

DATE:

_____

Children born
to a young man
are like sharp arrows
in a warrior's hands.
How happy is the
man whose quiver
is full of them!

PSALM 127:4, 5 NLT

WHAT A WONDERFUL LIFE
for
DADS

Standard
PUBLISHING
Bringing The Word to Life

Published by Standard Publishing
Cincinnati, Ohio
A division of Standex International Corporation
Printed in China
© Copyright 2005 Mark Gilroy Communications, Inc.
6528 E. 101st Street, Suite 416
Tulsa, Oklahoma 74133
www.markgilroy.com

Designed and illustrated by jacksondesignco, LLC
Springdale, Arkansas
www.jacksondesignco.com

ISBN 0-7847-1799-0

Acknowledgments

Nancy B. Gibbs wrote "A Dozen Character Traits Every Father Should Teach His Child" on page 68-69 and "The Future Begins Today" on page 37.

"When Daddy Says I'm Beautiful" is excerpted from a song of the same title by Annie Wolaver and Robin Wolaver. Copyright 2004 by Eb and Flo Music. Used by permission.

"Amazing Dads" on page 12-13 is adapted from Fact Monster/Information Please® Database, © 2005 Pearson Education, Inc.

Christy Philippe wrote "Hi There, Ugly?" on page 24-25, "What Does Your World Smell Like?" on page 27, "Father and Son on Par: Earl and Tiger Woods" on page 51, "Quality Time" on page 65, and "Lost!" on page 77.

Page 28 is adapted from *If There Is No God...* © 2001 by Mark Winter.

We found "A Father's Love" on page 88-89 in several places without attribution. Every effort was made to track down an original author. If you know where this material originated, we'd love it if you would contact us.

Table of Contents

There is no **greater** challenge than being a father **today**... and there is no greater joy than being a **father** today.

Introduction

A father's best gift to his children—and to himself—is his attitude of gratitude.

How often do you stop to think about how wonderful your life really is? *Do you really savor what it means to be a dad?*

No single attitude will change your outlook on life more profoundly and quickly than simple gratitude. Gratitude reminds you that even in the midst of challenges—conflict at work, not quite enough money in the checkbook, a discipline problem with a child—God's world is full of blessings and miracles, including your children! A thankful heart is a joyful heart.

As you read the following pages, let your heart and attitude be changed by a new sense of wonder that comes when you view life through the eyes of gratitude, optimism, and most importantly, faith in a loving God.

God looked over everything he had made; it was so good, so very good!

GENESIS 1:31 THE MESSAGE

The real voyage of discovery consists not in seeing new landscapes, but in having new eyes.

MARCEL PROUST

WHAT A WONDERFUL WORLD

LIFE IS WONDERFUL BECAUSE HE PUT THE STARS IN THE SKY
AND CREATED A WONDERFUL CHILD FOR YOU TO LOVE.

AMAZING DADS

Popular media stereotypes of fathers are not always flattering and often include humor that portrays lazy, uninterested dads. Some men have abrogated the responsibility to nurture their children, but a quick glance at any youth soccer field on a Saturday morning reveals many dads coaching and encouraging their kids.

Likewise, the animal kingdom has some committed and involved dads, too, which model the hard work and self-sacrifice of a loving father.

The duck: Male ducks tend to live as bachelors, but a number of duck breeds of North America help care for their young. *They must have discovered that even though the bachelor life may be easy in some ways, it gets awfully lonely!*

The wolf: When the mother wolf gives birth, the father stands guard outside their den and brings food for the mother and pups. As they grow, he plays with them and teaches them how to survive. Wolf families continue to live together much as human families do. *Male wolves—who don't have the best of reputations—need a better publicist.*

The marmoset: Father marmosets take care of the babies from birth. When a marmoset is born, the father cleans it, keeps it safe, and carries it to the mother only when it needs to be nursed. When the baby can eat solid food, it is the father who feeds the child. *Of course, they do feed them too much fast food!*

The penguin: A father emperor penguin shelters his eggs against icy winds for two months or more, holding them on his feet covered with a feathered flap. This committed dad doesn't eat the entire sixty days and loses about twenty-five pounds. When the chicks hatch, he feeds them a special liquid from his throat, stopping to eat and rest only after the mother comes to take charge. *Luckily for us, human mommies quickly take charge of baby care, although most of us could stand to lose a few pounds!*

The and grouse: A Namaqua sand grouse of Africa's Kalahari Desert flies fifty miles a day to soak himself in water so that his chicks can drink from his feathers when he returns to the nest. *Some of us drive our SUVs at least that much every day getting our kids to activities!*

All of creation is filled with wonderful dads—and aren't you glad you are one of them?

I love to think
of nature as an
unlimited broadcasting
station, through
which God speaks
to us every hour, if
we will only tune in.

GEORGE WASHINGTON CARVER

God's Wonders Are Both Tall and Wide

How unfathomable are the wonders of God's creation. For sheer volume, nothing can match the Amazon River. With over 80 inches of rainfall each year and more than a thousand tributary rivers, the Amazon is, on average, 130 feet deep and 25 miles across and holds two-thirds of all the flowing water in the world.

The earth indeed holds awesome depths—and heights. According to the *Guinness Book of World Records*, the world's most massive living tree is "General Sherman," a giant sequoia in California's Sequoia National Park, standing 275 feet tall with a trunk volume of 52,500 cubic feet.

But even more incredible than the wonders of God's creation is the wonder of his love—"Whether we are high above the sky or in the deepest ocean, nothing in all creation will ever be able to separate us from the love of God that is revealed in Christ Jesus our Lord" (Romans 8:39, NLT).

A Perfect World

*The more I study nature the more
I am amazed at the Creator.*

LOUIS PASTEUR

L ife is truly wonderful because of the world that God
created for us to inhabit.

The earth is tilted at 23.45 degrees—the perfect angle
to support life. Without the tilt to deflect the light and heat, the
earth would become too hot and water would build up in the
north and south poles.

The earth travels around the sun in an elliptical orbit at a
fairly constant speed. If our world slowed down, it would be
pulled so close to the sun at the narrow part of the orbit that
the earth would burn. If the earth orbited slightly more than
twice as fast as it does, it would break free from its orbit around
the sun, freezing us to death.

If the mass of our earth were only one-fourth less than it is, our atmosphere would be less dense and most of the planet would be an icy wasteland.

If the earth's crust were only ten feet thicker all the way around, the atmosphere would have less free oxygen.

If the earth were just 5% closer to the sun, the increased heat would melt the polar ice caps, raising the water level by as much as 300 feet.

If the earth rotated every 36 hours instead of every 24 hours, the temperature would roller coaster throughout the day, making life very uncomfortable, if not impossible.

Look at the night skies: Who do you think made all this? Who marches this army of stars out each night, counts them off, calls each by name—so magnificent! so powerful!—and never overlooks a single one?

ISAIAH 40:26 THE MESSAGE

A Walk in the Woods

To rekindle a sense of awe and wonder for God's wonderful world in your children's lives—and in your own life—plan a walk in the woods. You obviously need to consider the ages of your children when determining the kind of terrain you will explore and the distance of your walk. But get as far away from the ordinary as you can on a day trip. If your children are younger, provide them with a bag to "collect" things that interest them. They will love this part of your activity even if all they pick up are twigs and rocks. For older children and teens (and yourself), supply a journal. Toward the end of the day, set aside time to write down impressions of God's creation—and a prayer of thanksgiving to God for the world he has made.

Take time to marvel at the wonders of life.

GARY W. FENCHUK

The heavens declare
the glory of God;
the skies proclaim
the work of his hands.

PSALM 19:1

19

It is a **glorious** privilege
to live, to know, to act, to
listen, to behold, to **love**. To
look up at the blue summer
sky; to see the sun sink
slowly beyond the line of
the horizon; to **watch the**
worlds come twinkling into
view; first **one by one**, and
the myriads that no man can
count, and lo! The universe
is white with them; and
you and I are here.

MARCO MORROW

Lord,

You have created such a beautiful world. Just looking at a night sky, I'm amazed by the distance and beauty of the stars—the magnitude of your beautiful creation. Help me see your work anew today, God. Quicken my adoration for your creativity and might. Help me give my children a sense of awe of you, Lord God. Thank you for the wonderful world you've given us to live in.

*The Lord's delight is in those
who honor him, those who put
their hope in his unfailing love.*

PSALM 147:11 NLT

What God is
to the world,
parents are
to children.

PHILO

WHAT A WONDERFUL YOU

God made you—and your children—unique and special. Never forget how much you are loved.

Hi There, Ugly?

It is difficult to make a man miserable
while he feels worthy of himself and claims
kindred to the great God who made him.

ABRAHAM LINCOLN

It wasn't easy to pay attention in geometry. It was yearbook day, and so while the teacher droned on, we quietly signed books, passing them around the room.

I couldn't wait to get mine back. What would my friends say of me? When class was over, I quickly found my yearbook and flipped through it with anticipation. And then it caught my eye: Someone had written in big, bold letters across the inside cover of my book, HI THERE, UGLY!

I had never really considered myself good looking, but now it had been confirmed: I wasn't. If someone in the back of my geometry class thought I was ugly, there were probably many others who agreed. When I looked in the mirror, I realized the glaring truth: glasses, a few pimples, a big nose. The words in my yearbook were true.

Years went by. I married a very beautiful woman—both inside and out. I would tell her, "You're the most beautiful girl in the world!" and she would always reply, "And you're the most handsome man!" I never looked her in the eye when she said this. I would simply look at the ground and remember that the true verdict on my looks was tucked away in my seventh-grade yearbook.

Finally one day, she asked, "Why is it that you never look at me when I tell you that you're handsome?" I decided to come clean, and I told her about the yearbook incident. "That's crazy!" she replied. "I love you and I chose to marry you! And I think you're very handsome!"

It was the moment of truth: Whom was I going to believe—my wife, or some old graffiti in a yearbook?

I thought about that question for a long time and I chose to believe my wife—and God.

> *And as a bridegroom is happy in his bride,*
> *so your God is happy with you.*
>
> ISAIAH 62:5 THE MESSAGE

The **world** is a looking glass and gives back to **every man** the **reflection** of his own face. Frown at it and it will **in turn look** sourly upon you; **laugh** at it and with it, and it is a jolly, **kind companion.**

What Does Your World Smell Like?

Through the ages, wise men and philosophers have disagreed on many things, but many are in agreement on one point: We become what we think about. Ralph Waldo Emerson said, "A man is what he thinks about all day long." And in the Bible we read, "As a man thinks in his heart, so is he" (Proverbs 23:7).

One Sunday afternoon, a cranky grandfather was visiting his family. As he lay down to take a nap, his grandson decided to have a little fun by putting Limburger cheese on Grandfather's mustache. Soon, Grandfather awoke with a snort and charged out of the bedroom saying, "This room stinks." Through the house he went, finding every room smelling the same. Desperately he made his way outside only to find that "the whole world stinks!"

So it is when we fill our minds with negativism. Everything we experience and everybody we encounter will carry the scent we hold in our mind.

> *Whatever is true, whatever is noble, whatever is right, whatever is pure, whatever is lovely, whatever is admirable—if anything is excellent or praiseworthy—think about such things.*

> PHILIPPIANS 4:8

Your DNA determines everything about you, from your height to *eye* color to resistance to certain diseases. If the coded DNA instructions within one of your cells could be printed, the information would fill a thousand encyclopedia-sized books. God took great care in creating you—he must have had you in mind for a special purpose! Life becomes wonderful when you embrace God's plan and purpose for *you*!

Rabbi Zusya said that on the Day of Judgment, God would ask him, not why he had not been Moses, but why he had not been Zusya.

WALTER KAUFMANN

How Do I Love Me?

Though we need to honestly evaluate ourselves in order to grow and improve, it's easy to focus on our faults rather than our strengths. God wants us to be appropriately humble, but he doesn't want us to feed ourselves with crippling negativity. He wants us to love and respect ourselves. In your journal or on a blank sheet of paper, make a list of positive attributes God has given to you. Don't stop until you come up with at least twelve items on your list. Then write a prayer of thanksgiving that you are wonderfully made.

I would rather be what
God chose to make me
than the most glorious
creature that I could think
of; for to have been thought
about, born in God's
thought, and then made
by God, is the dearest,
grandest, and most
precious thing
in all thinking.

GEORGE MACDONALD

I praise
you because
I am fearfully and
wonderfully made;
your works are
wonderful, I know
that full well.

PSALM 139:14

Lord,

I stand in awe when I consider that you invite me to come before you as a friend. You, the creator of the universe, show me such amazing favor.

I will always speak your name with respect and reverence. I will always proclaim how great and mighty you are. I will always acknowledge that all good gifts are from you. I will always remember that I was created to serve you and for your pleasure. Help me instill in my children a love for you and respect for themselves.

You made me with a purpose and you are pleased with your creation. Thank you so much for considering me to be your friend, and for fulfilling your plans for me.

This is the day the Lord has made;
let us rejoice and be glad in it.

PSALM 118:24

My father used to play with
my brother and me in the yard.
Mother would come out and say,
"You're tearing up the grass."
"We're not raising grass," Dad
would reply. "We're raising boys."

HARMON KILLEBREW

34

WHAT A WONDERFUL CHALLENGE

LIFE IS WONDERFUL IN THE GOOD TIMES AND BAD TIMES.
SURE, BEING A FATHER CAN BE TOUGH AND IT TAKES SOME HARD
WORK—BUT OH, THE JOYS YOU EXPERIENCE ON THE WAY.

Life affords
no greater
responsibility,
no greater
privilege, than
the raising
of the next
generation.

C. EVERETT KOOP

The Future Begins Today

"Hey, Bob! Isn't your wife expecting a child?" the teacher asked. "She was when I left home," Bob replied, looking at the text message on his phone. "But not for much longer."

With those words, he jumped from his desk and took off to the hospital. Bob, unexpectedly a teenage father, had quit high school several years earlier to join the navy to support his family. Now done with his tour of duty, he knew that to support his family the way he would like to, he had to finish high school and start college. So Bob was attending high school for a final semester with much younger students—while expecting his second daughter!

When one of his classmates asked if he had any regrets, Bob's answer was: "I have definitely made some mistakes, but I know that my marriage, my children, my love for them, and God's love for me is no mistake at all. And if I have to work a little harder to get established than some men, then I am more than willing to do so. All any of us can do is start where we are!"

The Lord will fulfill his purpose for me.

PSALM 138:8

Lord, you will grant us peace, for all
we have accomplished is really from you.

ISAIAH 26:12 NLT

You have an amazing place in your child's

life—your kids need you! You're the one your kids look to for—

- Guidance: "Stand at the crossroads and look; ask for the ancient paths, ask where the good way is, and walk in it" (Jeremiah 6:16). Kids need the benefit of your experience and wisdom as they face important life decisions. That's right: Dads are the "ancient paths" of wisdom for our children.

- Encouragement: "Do not let any unwholesome talk come out of your mouths, but only what is helpful for building others up according to their needs, that it may benefit those who listen" (Ephesians 4:29). Dads have tremendous potential to make or break a child's self-image. Through verbally affirming and investing time and energy in your children, you show them that you love them. That puts them in a good position to face the world with confidence.

- Comfort: God "comforts us in all our troubles, so that we can comfort those in any trouble with the comfort we ourselves have received from God" (2 Corinthians 1:4). As fathers, God wants us to reach out in love and gentleness and touch the hearts of our kids.

- Vision: "Where there is no vision, the people perish" (Proverbs 29:18, *KJV*). Your kids need you to convey a positive outlook on their future. They need you to help them figure out what they're good at and express hope for future opportunities.

- Protection: "Stay here with me, and I will protect you with my own life" (1 Samuel 22:23, *NLT*). The world is full of physical, emotional, moral, and spiritual dangers—but dads can protect their kids by being a safe, involved, available presence in their lives.

As you endeavor to meet your children's needs, your day will be filled with challenges, opportunities, and adventures—and joy.

Success isn't accumulating possessions, wealth, or power. Success is obeying God. It means having those closest to you love and respect you the most.

JOHN C. MAXWELL

Amazing Feats

On June 30, 1859, Jean Francois Gravelet—alias Charles Blondin—made the earliest crossing of the Niagara Falls, walking across a three-inch rope 160 feet above the Falls with no assistance other than that of a long balancing pole.

Blondin didn't just walk daintily across the rope. On his first trip, he did a backwards somersault midway across. Each trip after that, he executed the walk across the Falls differently, crossing on stilts, blindfolded, pushing a wheelbarrow, with lit Roman candles attached to his pole, and sitting down to make an omelette. He even made a trip carrying his manager on his back.

Imagine what feats might be possible for you today as you trust God and take on the challenges before you!

Trust in the Lord with all your heart; do not depend on your own understanding. Seek his will in all you do, and he will direct your paths.

PROVERBS 3:5, 6 NLT

Somehow I can't **believe** that there are any heights that can't be scaled by a man who knows the **secrets** of making dreams come true. This **special** secret, it seems to me, can be summarized in four C's. They are curiosity, confidence, **courage**, and constancy, and the greatest of all is confidence. When you believe in a thing, **believe** in it all the way, implicitly and unquestionably.

WALT DISNEY

41

Job description for dads: Must be loving, strong, and good at jokes. Skills in ball throwing, hugging, and tickling a plus. Must expect long hours; pay is all the love you can hold.

AUTHOR UNKNOWN

Whatever you do, do well.

ECCLESIASTES 9:10 NLT

Balance

As men, we struggle with finding and creating ways to balance work, rest, play, and worship. It's hard to feel our best and give our best to family children when life gets out of whack.

Make a list for each category—*work*, *rest*, *play*, and *worship*—of two or three things you can do in each area to better achieve balance in your life this week and in the days ahead.

If this is a major struggle area for you, you might visit a local bookstore or library and select a book on priorities and time management—a classic like *7 Habits of Highly Successful People* is always in order—or do a simple Internet search and read some free articles on getting your life in harmony. Your goal is to find one principle for each category that you can put into practice today!

Time is the most valuable thing a man can spend.

LAERTIUS DIOGENES

Do all the good you can,
  By all the means you can,
In all the ways you can,
  In all the places you can,
At all the times you can,
  To all the people you can,
As long as you ever can.

JOHN WESLEY

Heavenly Father,

There is so much I want to accomplish today. You know my dreams and goals. Some of these aspirations are noble and worthy, while others, I confess, are superficial and spring out of my own selfishness.

Thank you, O God, for those dreams and goals that you have planted in my heart—and for giving me the wisdom to know which ones matter most. Help me to pursue them with your strength and direction.

But even more importantly, Father, help me to always press toward the greatest goal and greatest prize of all—to love you with all my heart. When I get caught up in my own plans, remind me through the Holy Spirit that the greatest prize of all is knowing you!

There are three things that will endure—faith, hope, and love—and the greatest of these is love.

1 CORINTHIANS 13:13 NLT

A truly rich man is one
whose children run
into his arms when
his hands are empty.

AUTHOR UNKNOWN

WHAT A WONDERFUL LOVE

YOUR LIFE BECOMES EVEN MORE WONDERFUL
AS YOU EXPRESS LOVE TO THE PEOPLE IN YOUR LIFE—
AND TEACH YOUR CHILDREN TO LOVE OTHERS.

You don't raise heroes; you raise sons.
And if you treat them like sons, they'll turn
out to be heroes, even if it's just in your own eyes.

WALTER SCHIRRA, SR.

Father and Son on Par: Earl and Tiger Woods

Tiger Woods has probably done more for the popularity of golf than any player in the history of the sport. But the charismatic young athlete might not be a household name today if not for his father and coach, Earl Woods.

Earl was born in Manhattan, Kansas on March 5, 1932, the youngest of six children. His childhood was filled with adversity, but, in his words, it made him the strong, focused person that he is today. In fact, the title of his book, *Playing Through*, is a play on the golf term for passing by a group of slower golfers on the same course. Earl's definition of playing through is "getting down to business and not letting anything stand in your way." That's how Earl Woods has lived his life and that's also the lesson he taught his son Tiger.

Tiger was born in California in 1975 and grew up to attend Stanford University. By the relatively young age of thirty, Tiger already achieved numerous PGA Tour and international victories. He was named 1996 PGA Rookie of the Year and 1997 PGA Player of the Year, among many other accolades.

Who can forget the emotional and heartfelt embrace between father and son after Tiger's extraordinary 1997 Masters victory? The hug said it all—showing the mutual respect, love, and admiration that the two of them share. President Clinton described the televised image of that father-and-son embrace as "the best shot of the day."

As testimony to this solid connection, Earl and Tiger don't believe in exchanging gifts on holidays like Father's Day. They feel it is enough just to celebrate their relationship.

To them, every day is Father's Day.

No one has seen God,
ever. But if we love one
another, God dwells
deeply within us, and his
love becomes complete
in us—perfect love!

1 JOHN 4:12
THE MESSAGE

What the World Needs Now

There are so many urgent and pressing needs in the world today.

- Work for the unemployed.
- Discipline for the indulgent.
- Goals for lost and wondering souls.
- Hope for the discouraged.
- Patience for the demanding.
- Peace for the troubled.

But the greatest need of all is God's love. And there's no better place to start spreading love than your own home.

*Each day of our lives we make deposits
in the memory banks of our children.*

CHARLES R. SWINDOLL

Why I Love Daddy Through the Years

Age 2 *Throw me way up high in the sky again, Daddy!*

Age 5 *Daddy helped me take the training wheels off my bike and reads stories to me.*

Age 8 *I went for ice cream with Daddy after my team lost. He said it's okay I struck out and I'll hit it next time.*

Age 12 *My daddy drove all six of us to the movie theater. We were laughing and screaming, but he didn't really say anything. He just had a funny expression on his face.*

Age 16 *His face was kind of red and then kind of white, but my dad was pretty cool about me backing the car into the garage door.*

Age 18 *I was kind of shocked to see my dad cry at graduation. Then I started crying too.*

Age 25 *Dad's still real funny. He's not old and boring like other kids' dads. He did complain about his back when he helped us move into our new place.*

Age 35 *Dad's got a lot of white in his hair. It's hard to think about him getting old.*

Age 45 *It's kind of nice to just sit around and talk with my dad like we're best friends.*

Age 55 *I love my daddy so much. I can't imagine a world without him in it.*

What a
father says
to his children
is not heard by
the world, but it
will be heard
by posterity.

YOU ARE FORGIVEN
AND I LOVE YOU

Several years ago, in Spain, a father named Juan had become estranged from his son, Paco. After over a year spent apart, Juan set off to find his son. He searched for months to no avail.

In a last, desperate effort to find him, the father put an ad in a Madrid newspaper. It read: *DEAR PACO, MEET ME IN FRONT OF THIS NEWSPAPER OFFICE AT NOON ON SATURDAY. YOU ARE FORGIVEN. I LOVE YOU. YOUR FATHER.*

On Saturday, 800 Pacos showed up, seeking forgiveness and love from their fathers.

A Date Day

Children spell "love" a little differently than adults: T - I - M- E. Plan an age-appropriate, kid-friendly "date" with your child for sometime in the next week. Don't rush the experience with strict time constraints, but savor every moment. If your child is younger, take him to a kids' movie or plan a park outing. If you have a teen, go shopping or out to lunch—or whatever you know she would love to do.

When Daddy Says I'm Beautiful

I remember five years old
Standing tiptoe at the window
Watching for my Daddy to get home
He always kisses Mama first
I lift my hands and beg my turn
He picks me up, a hug, a whirl
How's my beautiful baby girl?

When Daddy says I'm beautiful
He smiles with his eyes
And a happiness I can't describe
Fills me up inside
Confidence of love content within my soul
Even after he is gone and I am old

ANNIE WOLAVER
AND ROBIN WOLAVER

How great is
the love the Father
has lavished on us,
that we should be
called children of
God! And that
is what we are!

1 JOHN 3:1

Heavenly Father,

I can't imagine a greater love
than the love that I have for my children!
But Father, your infinite loving-kindness
is far beyond the finite love I can give
to my children. You guide and comfort me.
You always meet my needs. You are
my Father God. And you love me
as tenderly as a father!

Father,
I ask that you give me
words of encouragement for each
of my children. Help me today
to show them your love.

Teach your children to choose the right path, and when they are older, they will remain upon it.

PROVERBS 22:6 NLT

Nothing I've ever done
has given me more joys
and rewards than being
a father to my children.

BILL COSBY

62

WHAT A WONDERFUL RESPONSIBITY

THE BIRTH OF JOHN THE BAPTIST WAS ANNOUNCED
TO HIS FATHER BY AN ANGEL. BUT EVEN WITHOUT A
SPECIAL VISIT FROM AN ANGEL, EVERY FATHER KNOWS
GOD HAS ENTRUSTED HIM WITH A SPECIAL GIFT.

When you come **home** at night with only the shattered pieces of your **hopes and dreams**, he can mend them like new with two **magic words**—"Hi, Dad!"

Quality Time

During morning devotions with his two young daughters, Paul realized that he hadn't been spending as much time with his girls as he would like. After apologizing to them, he said, "You know, it's not always important the quantity of time we spend together, as it is the quality of time we spend together."

Julia, nine, and Emma, six, didn't quite understand.

Paul further explained, "Quantity means how much time, and quality means how good the times are that we spend together. Which would you rather have?"

Not missing a beat, Julia replied, "Quality time—and a lot of it!"

Dear children, let us stop just saying we love
each other; let us really show it by our actions.

1 JOHN 3:18 NLT

Do You Want to Be a Superdad?

Nothing makes life more wonderful for a family than a loving, caring, consistent husband and father. You can be a Superdad just by being a loving presence in your kids' lives (and you don't even have to wear a cape and tights). Here are a few areas to think about.

Do you effectively communicate love to your wife and children?

Does the way you interact with your kids tell them that you respect them, their opinions, and their emotions?

Do you balance security and spontaneity? Do you act with consistency and make your family feel secure, yet also plan with flexibility to bestow unexpected blessings on your kids?

Do you set a good example when it comes to responsibility? Do you follow through with work and home responsibilities? Do you plan ahead for emergencies and contingencies?

Do your children know that you're their biggest ally, their protector and advocate? Do you say only good things about them to others? Do you help them work through their problems?

Is your house a lighthearted place, where conversations are kind and respectful? Do your kids have fun at home? Do your family members feel that they can come home to rest and lighten their load?

The greatest gift I ever had
Came from God, and I call him Dad!
ANONYMOUS

67

A DOZEN CHARACTER TRAITS EVERY FATHER SHOULD TEACH HIS CHILD

Sometimes I wonder if my kids turned out as well as they did because of me or in spite of me. But there were things I made an effort to teach them while they were young. Somehow, I believe these twelve lessons helped them to become the responsible, caring young adults they are today.

- I taught my children that love is more important than anything else. We may not have always agreed, but love held our family together.
- I taught my children to be kind and respectful to those around them. *Please* and *thank you* were very important parts of their vocabulary.
- I taught my children that gratitude always followed blessings.
- I taught my children to study hard. I expected good grades, and, as one of my sons once commented, most kids live up to their parents' expectations.
- I taught my children to take care of the world around them. As a family, we worked in the yards together, raking and planting flowers.

- I taught my children that families have to work together toward common goals. When I went back to college, my wife and I had to work very hard, and each of my children had a part in keeping the house in order.

- I taught my children that worshipping God is not to be seen as an obligation, but as an honor and a privilege.

- I taught my children to appreciate what they had and not focus on the things they didn't have.

- I taught my children to be prompt. We may have had to rush around at times, but unless there was an emergency, we arrived at school before the tardy bell rang.

- I taught my children to appreciate the simple joys in life.

- I taught my children that the greatest blessings were those that were free. Playing ball in the front yard as a family, sharing lunch with the ducks at the pond, and watching television together were times that I will always remember.

- I taught my children to forgive and forget. Holding grudges wasn't an option in our house.

As parents, we want our kids to grow into respectable young adults ready to face the world with a sense of happiness in their hearts. A father blesses his children's lives—and his own life is blessed—when he takes the responsibility to teach them.

ROY GIBBS

To Do!

Life Is a Gift

One of the lost arts of civility
and friendship is the hand-
written note. Take time today to
write several thank-you notes.
Write notes to your spouse,
your own parents, friends who
have been an encouragement
to you, and yes, even a hand-
written note to your child!

God gave you
a gift of 86,400
seconds today.
Have you used
one to say
thank you?

WILLIAM A. WARD

Children are a
gift from the
Lord; they are a
reward from him.

PSALM 127:3 NLT

Dear Heavenly Father,

*Thank you for the gift of my children.
I'm grateful, God, for every picture on my
refrigerator and in my office, for the privilege
of sharing in their accomplishments,
for the love they bring to my life.*

*God, I'm amazed that you've entrusted to me
these precious lives. Lord, I give them over to
you and pray that you would guide each day of
their lives. Thank you for the opportunity to help
them grow into strong young people who love
you. Please give me wisdom to share and daily
gratitude for this amazing gift.*

I know what I'm doing.
I have it all planned out—
plans to take care of you,
not abandon you,
plans to give you the
future you hope for.

JEREMIAH 29:11
THE MESSAGE

Everyone's future is,
in reality, uncertain and
full of unknown treasures
from which all may
draw unguessed prizes.

LORD DUNSANY

WHAT A WONDERFUL FUTURE

LIFE IS WONDERFUL TODAY—BECAUSE WE ALSO HAVE THE HOPE OF WONDERFUL TOMORROWS. OUR KIDS WILL GROW AND MATURE—AND GOD IS STILL WORKING ON YOU AS WELL!

Walk boldly and wisely. There is a hand above that will help you on.

PHILIP JAMES BAILEY

Lost!

A father once took his little son for a walk in the woods. As they were walking along hand in hand, they stopped for a moment, and the father asked, "Do you know where we are?"

The little boy said, "No!"

"Do you know where we're going?" the father asked.

Again, the little boy said, "No!"

The father chuckled and said, "Well, I guess you're lost then!"

The boy looked up at his father and said, "No, I'm not lost. I'm with you!"

The Lord keeps watch over you as you
come and go, both now and forevermore.

PSALM 121:8 NLT

A Bright Future

My purpose is to give life in all its fullness.

JOHN 10:10 NLT

Life doesn't feel wonderful when we allow the clouds of fear and doubt to trouble our hearts. The good news is that God secures our future.

- He replaces uncertainty with the promise of good days (see Jeremiah 29:11).
- He provides peace in the midst of storms (see John 14:27).
- He hears our prayers (see 1 John 5:14).
- He quells worry with his peace (see Philippians 4:7).
- He promises us an eternal home (see Revelation 21:3).

Smile. Trust God for your—and your child's—future.

Life is God's novel. Let him write it.

ISAAC BASHEVIS SINGER

79

I am not
afraid of
tomorrow, for
I have seen
yesterday
and I love
today.

WILLIAM ALLEN WHITE

*I will not leave
you as orphans;
I will come to you.*

JOHN 14:18

A Wonderful Goal

People who articulate their dreams, goals, and plans tend to be more successful at achieving desired results and feeling a sense of purpose. What are some of the dreams and goals you have for your life? How can you help instill a sense of purpose in the lives of your children?

Write down four or five major goals. List one that could be accomplished in the next year and another that could take several years. Under each goal, write down three or four very specific action steps.

If your children are in their teen years, work with them on doing the same activity for themselves. If you have young school-age children, try a very directed activity of helping them state one very specific and attainable "future" goal—such as a new bike—and give them a few tasks to help achieve that goal.

There is **one thing** that gives radiance to everything. It is **the idea** of something around the corner.

G. K. CHESTERTON

83

God has not **promised** skies always blue, flower-strewn **pathways** all our lives through; God has not promised sun without rain, **joy without sorrow**, peace without pain. But **God has promised** strength for the day, rest for the labor, **light for the way**, **grace for the trials**, help from above, unfailing sympathy, **undying love.**

KRISTONE

Father God,

Thank you for all the ways you've shown yourself to be trustworthy. Over and over again in my life, you've taken care of me and my family. You've challenged and enabled me; you've comforted and uplifted me. And you've promised to keep taking care of me today and tomorrow and the day after that.

Thank you for the future you have planned for me and my children. Please fill my heart with joy today as I remember that you— and your plans—are good!

The Lord is like a father
to his children, tender
and compassionate
to those who fear him.

PSALM 103:13 NLT

God, having you for my father
is the best thing that could have
ever happened in my life.
Thank you for letting me
be in your family.

JONI EARECKSON TADA

WHAT A WONDERFUL GOD

THE REAL REASON THAT LIFE IS WONDERFUL IS
BECAUSE THAT'S THE WAY GOD CREATED IT TO BE. YOUR
LIFE IS RICHER WHEN YOU SAY THANKS TO THE GIVER OF ALL
GOOD GIFTS—ESPECIALLY FOR THE GIFT OF YOUR CHILDREN!

A Father's Love

A very wealthy man and his son shared a passion for art collecting. Together they traveled around the world, adding priceless works by Picasso, Van Gogh, Monet, and many masters.

As war engulfed the nation, the young man left to serve his country. After only a few short weeks, his father received devastating news—his beloved son had died while rushing a fellow soldier to a medic.

Distraught and lonely, the old man faced the upcoming Christmas holidays with anguish and sadness.

On Christmas morning, a knock on the door awakened the depressed old man. He was greeted by a soldier holding a large package who said, "I was the one your son was rescuing when he died." The soldier went on to tell of how the son had told everyone about his father's love of fine art.

"I am an artist," said the soldier, "and I want to give you this." The old man unwrapped the package to find a portrait of his son. Though it would never be considered a masterpiece, the painting featured the young man's face in striking detail. The man gave the soldier his heartfelt thanks.

The following spring, the old man became ill and passed away. Soon after, an auction house buzzed with anticipation as the man's paintings came up for sale—starting with the painting of his son.

"Who will open the bidding with $100?" the auctioneer asked. Minutes passed, and no one spoke.

The auctioneer insisted that, per the collector's wishes, the portrait had to be sold before any other paintings. Finally, a neighbor of the old man spoke. "Will you take ten dollars for the painting? That's all I have. I knew the boy, so I'd like to have it."

When no one contested the bid, the gavel fell, and the painting was awarded to the neighbor.

Cheers filled the room and someone exclaimed, "Now we can get on with it and we can bid on the real treasures!"

The auctioneer looked at the audience and announced that the auction was over.

Stunned disbelief quieted the room. Someone spoke up and asked, "What about all of these paintings? There is millions of dollars worth of art here!"

The auctioneer replied, "It's very simple. According to the will of the father, whoever takes the son...gets it all."

Thank God for his Son—a gift too wonderful for words!

2 CORINTHIANS 9:15 NLT

A Heart Like Joseph's

*An angel of the Lord appeared to him in a
dream and said, "Joseph son of David, do not be
afraid to take Mary home as your wife, because
what is conceived in her is from the Holy Spirit. She
will give birth to a son, and you are to give him the name
Jesus, because he will save his people from their sins."*

MATTHEW 1:20, 21

We know a little about his family tree. The Gospel of Matthew tells us that Joseph's ancestry included such luminaries as David, Solomon, and Hezekiah.

We know his occupation was carpentry. And though the Bible doesn't tell us specifically, we surmise that Joseph died sometime after Jesus' twelfth birthday, as he is never mentioned beyond that point.

Perhaps the most important fact we know about Joseph is that he was a man of character and faith who obeyed God.

He protected Mary's sexual purity throughout their engagement. When he learned that Mary was pregnant, it was certain: he was *not* the father.

He showed mercy to Mary. He chose not to humiliate her in public even though she appeared to have been unfaithful.

After the angel spoke to him, Joseph obeyed the Lord by taking Mary home as his wife. In those extraordinary circumstances, Joseph chose to do right, and his reward was being Jesus' earthly father.

Joseph's remarkable faith and obedience to God truly set him apart. We can create a wonderful life for our families and ourselves when we demonstrate the same godly character. Why not start today?

Be cheerful no matter what; pray all the time; thank God no matter what happens. This is the way God wants you who belong to Christ Jesus to live.

1 THESSALONIANS 5:16-18
THE MESSAGE

Prayer puts God's work in his hands— and keeps it there.

E.M. BOUNDS

Whatever we do, even if we are reading the Word or praying, we should stop for a few minutes—as often as possible—to praise God from the depths of our hearts, to enjoy him there in secret. Since you believe that he is always with you, no matter what you may be doing, why shouldn't you stop for awhile to adore him, to praise him, to petition him, to offer him your heart, and to thank him?

BROTHER LAWRENCE,
THE PRACTICE OF THE
PRESENCE OF GOD

Count Your Blessings

What do you have to be thankful to God for? Make a list of God's blessings in the last week, month, and year (for example: your children and wife, meeting your material needs, lifting your spirits at opportune times). Then write a note of thanks to God and tuck it in your Bible for future reference.

Gratitude
is happiness
doubled by
wonder.

G.K. CHESTERTON

A Prayer for a Dad's Heart

If God cares so wonderfully for flowers that are here today
and gone tomorrow, won't he more surely care for you?

MATTHEW 6:30

Dear Heavenly Father,

*I can get so caught up in my needs and problems that I
sometimes forget that you are the giver of all good gifts
and that you know—and meet—all my needs.*

*I know that I don't have all the answers, but I choose to
live with confidence and faith because you promise to
give me exactly what I need each day.*

Amen.